The Antarctic

The story of the Antarctic is a story of human endurance. The early explorers who forced a passage through the icy seas to the continent beyond had to fight for their survival. Some, like Captain Scott, lost that fight. Today, scientists and biologists equipped with modern instruments and protected vehicles still find the biting cold and fierce Antarctic storms a gruelling experience. This book will tell you about modern studies of ice movements and currents, and show you some of the strange and beautiful marine life. The future looks exciting. Beneath those glassy seas there could be oil and natural gas; icebergs could be towed to drought-ridden areas to provide water; and before long some of us may be lucky and brave enough to take a pleasure cruise around the Antarctic islands. Look at the back of the book for a glossary and a list of books which might interest you.

SEAS AND OCEANS

The Antarctic

Edited by Pat Hargreaves

WAYLAND

SILVER BURDETT

© Copyright 1980 Wayland Publishers Ltd
First published in 1980 by
Wayland (Publishers) Limited
61 Western Road, Hove,
East Sussex BN3 1JD, England

Published in the United States by
Silver Burdett Press
Morristown, New Jersey
1987 printing

Phototypeset by
Trident Graphics Limited, Reigate, Surrey
Printed in Italy by
G. Canale & C. S.p.A., Turin

Library of Congress Cataloging-in-Publication Data

The Antarctic.

(Seas and oceans)
Bibliography: p. [72].
Includes index.
Summary: Depicts the geological history, discovery and exploration, plant and animal life, and resources of Antarctica, and discusses treaties pertaining to it. Includes a glossary.
1. Antarctic regions–Juvenile literature. [1. Antarctic regions]
I. Hargreaves, Pat. II. Series.
G863.A57 1986   910'.09167   86-29817
ISBN 0-382-06467-4 (Silver Burdett)

Seas and Oceans

Three-quarters of the earth's surface is covered by sea. Each book in this series takes you on a cruise of a mighty ocean, telling you of its history, discovery and exploration, the people who live on its shores, and the animals and plants found in and around it.

The Atlantic
The Caribbean and Gulf of Mexico
The Mediterranean
The Antarctic
The Arctic
The Indian Ocean
The Red Sea and Persian Gulf
The Pacific

Contents

1 A JOURNEY AROUND THE SOUTH POLE

The South Pole, the 'end of the earth', lies in a great icy continent called Antarctica, which is as large as the United States of America and Europe put together, and twice the size of Australia. The coastline of Antarctica is 22,400 kilometres (14,000 miles) around its edge. Most of the land lies within the Antarctic Circle, a line of latitude which you can see on the map on page 35.

Antarctica is surrounded by the Antarctic Seas which make up the Antarctic Ocean. The Pacific, Indian and Atlantic Oceans all meet at the Antarctic. Both the ocean and the continent are extremely cold. There are ice mountains, glaciers and snow covering the land all the year round. In summer some of this melts, but even so nearly all the land remains blanketed in ice. In some areas, huge ice shelves are formed where the land and sea join. These are so thick that it is possible to travel over them, and use heavy equipment. At the sea edge, these ice shelves form great ice cliffs. Sea ice and enormous floating icebergs are found in the ocean near the land and also way

Below The glaciers and snow-clad mountains of Antarctica slope down to an icy sea.

Above Newly-formed sea ice at McMurdo Sound. Huge areas of sea-water around the Antarctic freeze over during the long winter.

out to sea. These make journeys by ship dangerous.

Antarctica can also be called the 'Land of the Midnight Sun'. On Midsummer Day (which in this part of the world occurs in December) at the Antarctic Circle there is sunlight for twenty-four hours; at the Pole itself there are six months of daylight. In winter there are long, long periods without any sun at all.

Look at the map. First find the Falkland Islands, where people live and farm the land.

Then pin-point the Antarctic Continent and the South Pole. You will also see the Ross Sea and the Weddell Sea. Between the land and the Ross Sea is a huge ice shelf (the Ross Ice Shelf). On the edge of the ice shelf, about 4,000 kilometres (2,500 miles) from the coast of New Zealand, is the Bay of Whales. Where the ice shelf meets the land you will see McMurdo Sound, where there is a large scientific base. The Ross Sea and the Ross Ice Shelf are named after Captain James Clark Ross.

Above A cartoonist's idea of how early British expeditions made merry during a long Antarctic winter. The reality was very different.

Below H.M.S. *Endurance*, an ice patrol boat, steams through pack-ice four metres thick.

Antarctica was first sighted by British seamen and a Russian admiral in 1820. Captain Cook had crossed the Antarctic Circle before this but never saw the land beyond the pack ice. If any land did exist he thought it would be of 'inexpressibly horrid aspect . . . doomed by nature never to feel the warmth of the sun's rays, but to lie for ever buried under snow and ice'. Some explorers who have trekked to the South Pole since Cook's time have often agreed with him, but Antarctica is also a place of wonder and excitement. Captain Ross, who saw the range of snow and ice-clad mountains along the western border of the Ross Sea, thought it 'a scene of grandeur and magnificence far beyond anything we had before seen or could have conceived'.

The first people to spend a winter on Antarctica were a party of ten from a British expedition which reached the continent in a ship called the *Southern Cross* in 1899. They were also the first to sledge on the Ross Ice Shelf. Sixteen kilometres (10 miles) south of the Bay of Whales, a part of this Shelf where the ice cliffs are low, they saw level ice extending southwards as far as they could see. Twelve years later a Norwegian explorer, Roald Amundsen, took this route to the Pole, and in 1933–5 the area became the site of 'Little America', the camp of Admiral Byrd.

Over the years scientists and other experts have studied the rocks, ice and plants of the Antarctic, and the birds and animals that nest or breed there. Recently, expeditions have been looking at the incoming radiations of the sun and their effects on the atmosphere. They have also studied the possible effects of ice movements and melting ice on the sea level and climate all over the world.

In this book you will find out more about the discoveries of explorers and scientists. But you should also read the diaries of those who have lived on Antarctica, sheltering from frightful cold and storms during journeys by sea, on foot or even in today's well-protected snow vehicles. Those long winter nights are grim indeed, but in the strong light of a fine summer day or in the varying colours of the midnight sun, Antarctica is a grand and magnificent place.

Above Scientists take water samples through a hole in the sea ice.

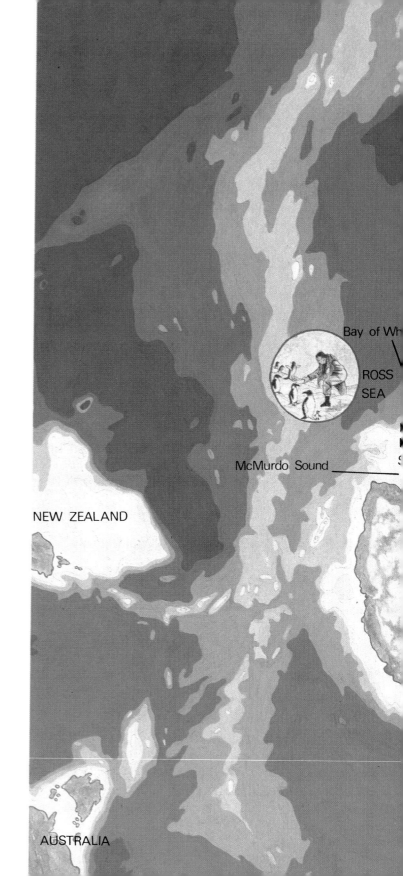

Right Map of Antarctica and the Antarctic Ocean.

Bay of Wh

ROSS
SEA

McMurdo Sound

NEW ZEALAND

AUSTRALIA

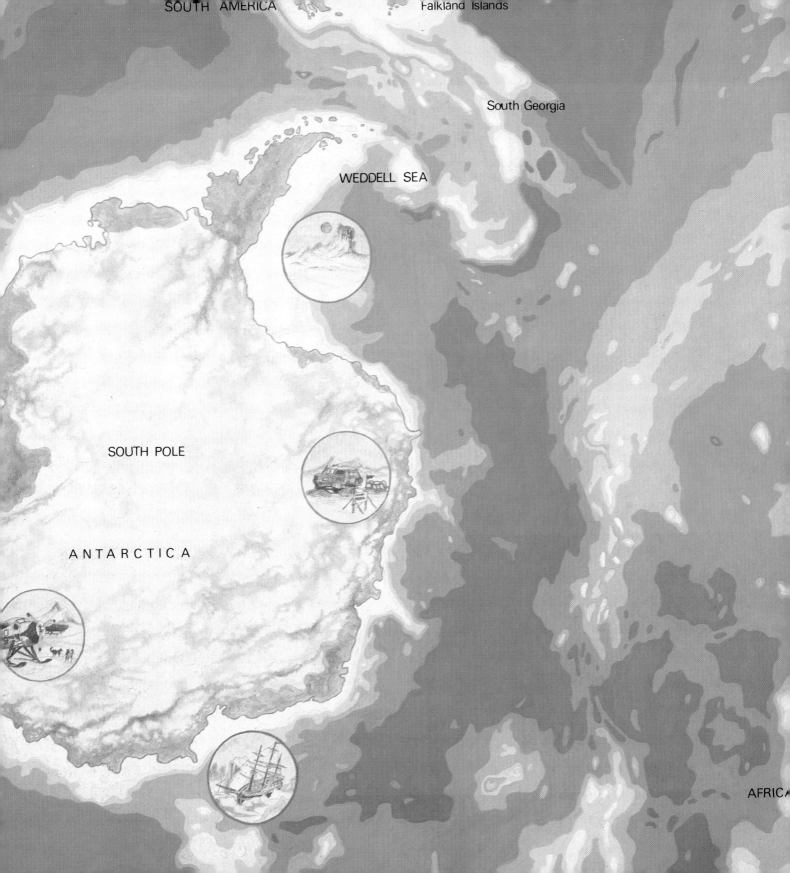

SOUTH AMERICA   Falkland Islands

South Georgia

WEDDELL SEA

SOUTH POLE

ANTARCTICA

AFRICA

2 THE BIRTH OF THE ANTARCTIC OCEAN

Continental drift

Compared with the age of the Earth, the Antarctic Ocean is very young. Long ago, there was a gigantic continent over the South Pole. It consisted of Antarctica, South America, Africa, India, Australia and New Zealand all joined together. This giant continent was called Gondwanaland. Geologists who have studied this area have found identical types of rocks in all of the southern continents. There is also evidence of an ancient ice age which affected them all.

130 million years ago, Gondwanaland began to break up, and the outer parts of it, which are now South America, Africa and India began to move away from the central block, which became Antarctica. Australia and New Zealand broke away later. Gradually the cracks widened, and molten rock, or lava, rose up from inside the earth to fill them. But the lava was heavier than the rocks which formed the continents, so it did not rise so high; the higher continents were 'floating' on the heavier material beneath them. The lava-filled valleys widened and deepened, until they were so deep that the sea could flow in, and the Antarctic Ocean was born.

Gradually, over millions of years, the Antarctic Ocean has widened and the continents on either side have continued to separate. The lava which filled the original cracks became firmly joined to the continental rocks, but new cracks formed in this solidified lava,

and these in their turn were filled with fresh lava. Thus a band of solidified lava gradually grew up between the pieces of broken continent. This solidified lava is now the sea floor, and new cracks still form in it and are still filled with fresh lava. This happens along a line in the middle of the ocean.

Right The Antarctic sea-bed. If the ocean were drained of water, this is what it would look like.

Below Ash and lava from a volcanic eruption form a giant cloud off the coast of Antarctica in 1968. This eruption formed a new island which rose sixty metres out of the sea.

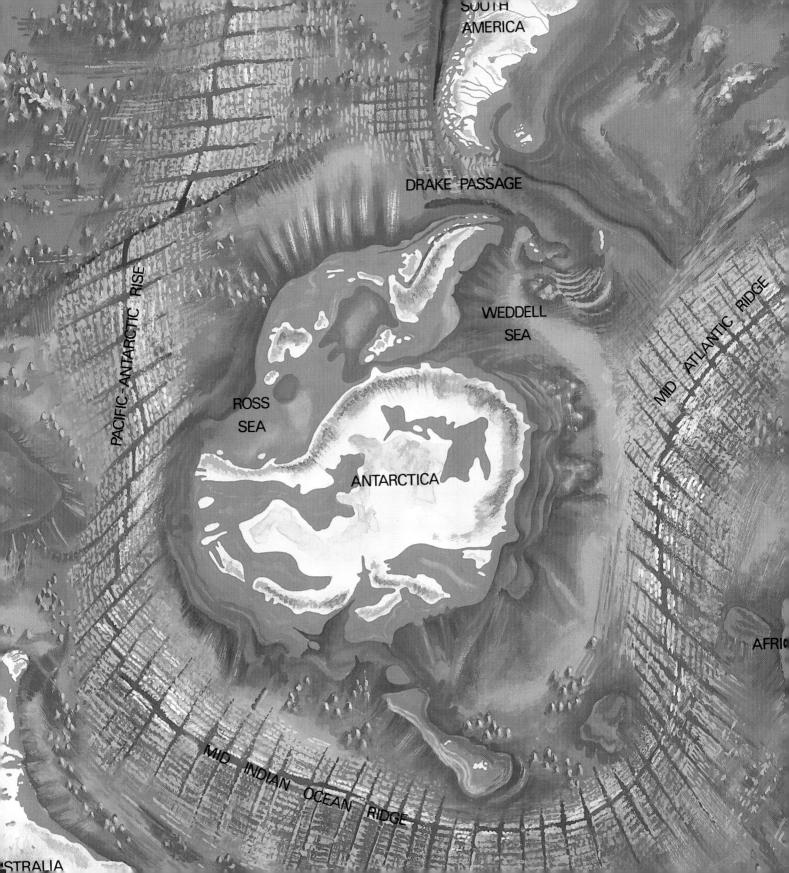

SOUTH
AMERICA

DRAKE PASSAGE

WEDDELL
SEA

PACIFIC-ANTARCTIC RISE

MID ATLANTIC RIDGE

ROSS
SEA

ANTARCTICA

AFRIC

MID INDIAN OCEAN RIDGE

STRALIA

14

Continental shelves and slopes

If we were to take an imaginary journey along the sea floor from the edge of the land out into the middle of the ocean basin, we would discover a fascinating landscape. Near the land, the ice-covered water would be shallow – in fact we would be on the continental shelf, which is really still part of the continent. The sea here is shallow and if sea-level were to fall a hundred metres (as it does during ice ages when a lot of water is locked up on land as ice) the continental shelf would be uncovered and become dry land. The surface of the continental shelf is quite flat and smooth, and marine life is plentiful.

Moving out towards the edge of the continental shelf, we would notice some small valleys. These are caused by sand and mud being swept off the edge of the continental shelf. As the sand passes over the sea floor, it gradually cuts out valleys. Beyond the edge of the continental shelf, the sea floor would slope down steeply in front of us. This steep region is called the continental slope. Here the valleys have deepened to become impressive canyons. We might see small trickles of sand falling down some of them. On rare occasions they carry great masses of gravel, sand and mud down toward the deep sea floor. The water then rushes past, and stones and mud tumble down in a great torrent. These rare events are called 'turbidity currents'.

If we continued our journey down the continental slope, we would see ridges and valleys ahead of us, remains of the earth movements

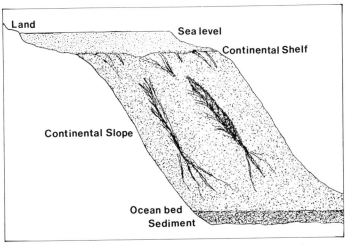

Above The continental shelf, near the land, is the shallowest part of the sea floor. Beyond the edge of the shelf, the sea-bed slopes steeply down towards the bottom of the ocean.

which took place when Gondwanaland originally split apart. Eventually, however, we would reach the bottom of the continental slope and find ourselves on the floor of the deep Antarctic Ocean itself. Here again the sea floor is fairly flat and smooth, and covered with fine mud. However, at intervals, we would see ranges of hills rising out of the mud, and occasionally extinct volcanoes. There would be a few marine animals, but not so many as there are on the shallow shelf. The water down here is very cold and dark.

Far left Marine life is most plentiful on the continental shelf.

Rocks and sediments

Where does all the sediment – the mud and sand – on the sea floor come from? Well, on the continental shelf and slope, and on the deep sea floor near the foot of the slope, most of it comes from the land. In the Antarctic, glaciers are continuously sliding across the rocks on land towards the sea. The glaciers' movement gradually grinds down the rocks into smaller and smaller pieces: gravel, sand, silt and mud. When the glacier reaches the sea, this loose material is deposited on the continental shelf.

Below Scientists trawl for rock samples from the sea floor off the the coast of South Georgia.

But it does not stay there. Currents gradually wash it across the continental shelf and down into the deep ocean basin. The finest material can be moved most easily, and travels farthest, whereas coarse gravels can only be moved by the strongest currents and tend to stay near the shore.

There is, however, another source of sediments. When sea creatures die, their bodies sink to the bottom of the sea. The largest part of the sediments on the deep sea floor is made up of the skeletons of microscopic (very tiny) creatures. When these creatures first fall to the sea floor they accumulate as layers of soft material called 'ooze'. But they are gradually pressed down by their own weight until they finally form rocks such as chalk and limestone.

The skeletons of these creatures are preserved in the rocks, as fossils. Fossils are very important to geologists, because they help date the rocks. The animals and plants we know today have not always lived on the Earth. In the past, there were different types of creatures. Over thousands or millions of years, one type evolves into another. That means it adapts its shape or other characteristics to suit the changing environment. Geologists have been able to work out the order in which different creatures evolved, and the times when they were living. So, if we find a rock or sediments with fossils in it, and if the fossils can be recognized, we know that the rock in which they are found was formed at the time when that type of creature was living.

Above An ammonite – the fossil of an extinct sea creature – found on the sea-bed of the Antarctic Ocean.

3 ICE ON LAND, ICE AT SEA

Ice ages

You have all seen sheets of ice on ponds or on lakes. When the temperature rises, the ice melts. However, if the temperature never rose enough to melt the ice from the previous winter, a permanent sheet of ice would remain. This is what happens on a larger scale during an ice age. At the Poles, the ice sheet grows thicker until it moves under its own weight. On mountains, the ice forms huge glaciers that flow down valleys until they melt at lower and warmer levels. If the glaciers still do not melt before reaching flat country, they expand into a vast ice sheet that spreads to the coast and grows towards the Equator until it does melt.

During an ice age, water no longer returns to the oceans in rivers, but freezes and forms ice sheets. Only 18,000 years ago, the ice sheets in the northern hemisphere were nearly twice the volume of the present Antarctic ice sheet. This made sea level in the world some 100 metres (330 ft) lower than it is today. Britain was linked to Europe because the North Sea dried out; Australia was joined to New Guinea, and Alaska to Siberia. Large areas of dry land also appeared in the South China Sea, the Gulf of Mexico and off Arctic North America and Siberia. Look on a map of the world to help you imagine what this would be like.

Nowadays, the ice on the Antarctic continent has an average thickness of about 2,000 metres (6,600 ft), which is higher than most mountains in warmer countries. Do you live near a port? If all the ice in Antarctica were to melt, sea level would rise by about 65 metres (212 ft). This would be sufficient to flood all the world's sea ports and vast areas of low-lying land. Even if one-tenth of the ice in Antarctica slid off into the sea, sea level would rise by six metres (20 ft), and that is enough to cause great damage to the world's coastlines.

Right Snow and ice-clad mountains and glaciers cover the Antarctic continent all the year round.

Below This fjord in Norway was once a valley on dry land. It was 'drowned' by the rising sea-level, following the shrinking of the Antarctic and Arctic ice sheets after the last ice age.

Ice and the Antarctic Ocean

In warmer countries, crops, trees and bare land, readily absorb most of the heat of the sun's rays. However, the cold, dry snow and ice of Antarctica reflect most of this heat back into space. Being higher and colder than other continents, the surface of the Antarctic ice sheet does not melt except near the coast. This makes it the coldest continent in the world, with average yearly temperatures reaching $-60°C$.

The cold Antarctic Ocean also affects the climate further north. You need to be some 500 kilometres (300 miles) closer to the Equator in the southern hemisphere than in the northern hemisphere to experience the same temperature.

Below Some icebergs are hollowed and sculptured into fantastic shapes by the buffeting of the sea.

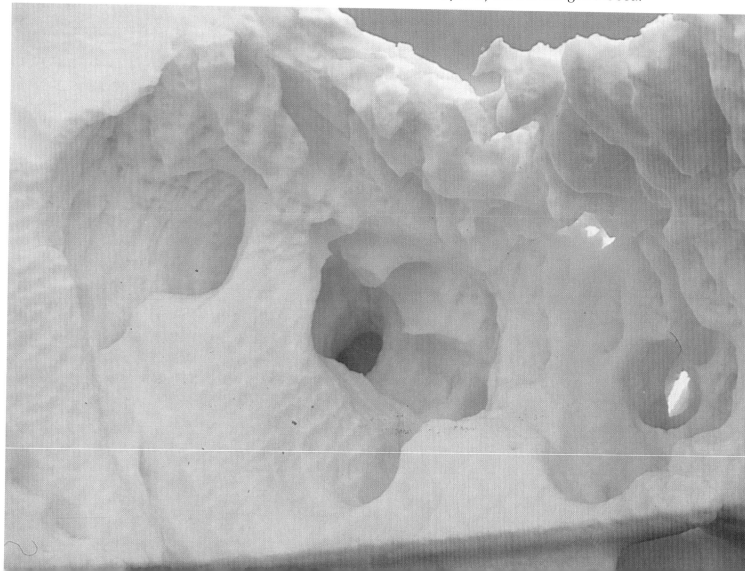

Above Ice cliffs at the Bay of Whales on the Ross Ice Shelf.

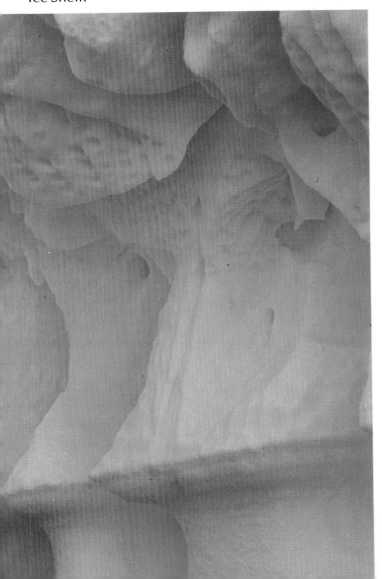

Sea water, even if only a degree or two above freezing point, melts ice very quickly. Many glaciers therefore finish at sea level. However, Antarctica is so cold that its ice sheet has spread over the shallower, surrounding seas. Much of it also rests on the sea bed near the sea shore, as the ice does not float until the sea is at least 200 metres (660 ft) deep.

Around parts of the continent, the ice forms vast, floating ice shelves. The Ross Ice Shelf, the largest of these, is about as big as Spain. It prevents ships from getting any nearer the coast at this point. Early explorers had to sledge over the ice shelf to reach the South Pole. Movements of the sea, due to tides and storms, sometimes break off icebergs from the ice shelves. The shelves themselves are 'fed' by glaciers that erode valleys in the surrounding mountains on land. Because of this, the ice shelves and the icebergs are made up of frozen fresh water.

Huge areas of sea water around the Antarctic continent also freeze over to a thickness of between half a metre and three metres (1.5 to 10 ft). In sheltered, coastal waters near the land, this ice remains fixed and is called 'fast ice'. Further out to sea, where it drifts with winds and tides, it is called 'pack-ice'. Near the open sea, waves, swell and warmer temperatures in the summer months break the pack-ice into 'floes'. These can be quite small but may be thousands of metres across. Fast ice, pack-ice and ice floes are all made up of frozen sea-water.

Above Scott's ship H.M.S. *Discovery* was unable to break out of the fast ice in McMurdo Sound in the summer of 1902–1903.

Icebergs are also found drifting among the pack-ice. Some of these are flat on top. They are called tabular icebergs and range in size from one kilometre or less to over one hundred kilometres across (half a mile to 160 miles). Such huge icebergs are a unique feature of Antarctic waters. Other icebergs are fantastically hollowed and carved into grotesque shapes by the buffeting of the sea. It has been estimated that the largest iceberg contains enough fresh water to supply the needs of London for 700 years. Some people are studying the possibility of towing huge icebergs to dry countries, such as those in the Middle East, to provide water for drinking and irrigation. Most of an iceberg in fact lies below sea level and it is only a small proportion that can be seen above the surface.

Specially strengthened ships are needed for ice-covered waters. Early explorers often had

Above Ice floes in the Weddell Sea, as seen from the bows of a research ship. A huge tabular iceberg stretches away on the horizon.

their wooden sailing ships badly damaged while breaking through the pack-ice. Sometimes their ships would be jammed fast between two floes, and the crews would be forced to drift around the continent with the ice. Today a strengthened ship of a few hundred tonnes can force a passage through relatively loose pack-ice fairly easily. For solid fast ice and heavier pack-ice, larger and more powerful ships – icebreakers – are needed. Icebreakers can keep moving in ice of one or two metres (3 to 6 ft) thick and break thicker ice more gradually.

United States' icebreakers cut a channel through fast ice into McMurdo Sound each year to take supplies to their main base. At this site in the summer of 1902–3, Scott's ship *Discovery* was unable to break out of the fast ice. The following year it did escape, but only with a struggle.

4 THE FIRST EXPLORERS

For thousands of years, people wondered about the existence of a strange southern land. In the great age of exploration after the discovery of America, European nations raced each other in the search for a great continent, which was believed to exist in the southern oceans. 'It was', the explorer Quiros wrote in 1605, 'a land of gold and silver, cattle and grain, the richest fruit and the healthiest climate.' It took many years for this dream to die.

Indeed, it was not until the voyages of Captain James Cook in the 1770s, that the mystery of the southern continent was finally laid to rest. Cook was the first to cross the Antarctic Circle and glimpse the ice fields surrounding the continent. He judged that the land beyond would be quite uninhabitable and

Below Dog teams were vital for hauling supplies on early expeditions. Here a sledging party return to their ship at the Bay of Whales.

of no use to anyone. However, he did find the Antarctic Ocean rich in whales and seals, and for the next half century, its frozen wastes were exploited by hunters out to make their fortunes from the fur trade.

In the 1830s and 1840s there were a number of voyages aimed at scientific discovery and exploration. A British expedition, led by Captain James Ross, worked its way through 160 kilometres (100 miles) of pack-ice to reach the Ross Sea. Ross was prevented from going any further south by an ice barrier (the Ross Ice Shelf) between 50 and 75 metres (165 and 245 ft) high, and spanning the water as far as the eye could see. Ross sailed eastward looking for a way round, but wrote that he might just as well try to sail through the cliffs of Dover! (Captain Scott was later to look over the Ross Ice Shelf from a balloon.) One of the most astonishing discoveries of Ross's voyage was Mount Erebus, an active volcano in this otherwise silent and icy wasteland.

It was not until the turn of this century that a determined attempt was made to cross the Antarctic continent itself. Ernest Shackleton was the first to reach the 3,000-metre (10,000 ft) high polar plateau that led towards the South Pole, on an expedition in 1908. Captain Robert Scott later described it as 'so wildly and awfully desolate that it cannot fail to impress one with gloomy thoughts'. These early sledging journeys were both difficult and dangerous. Where glaciers from the mountains and the plateau force their way into the ice shelves, there are

Above Aerial view of the mountain range leading up to the 3,000 metre-high polar plateau.

Below This 'husky' dog finds it hard to keep his head above the snow drifts during a blizzard.

many crevasses, through which it was difficult to find a way. Severe cold, blizzards and drifting snow sapped the explorers' strength, and they could never take enough food for such heavy work as sledge-hauling. Expeditions were forced to eat their ponies and dogs, as food ran out.

In 1911 the race for the South Pole began in earnest. Three years earlier, Shackleton had fought his way to within 155 kilometres (97 miles) of the Pole, but had been forced to turn back. Now two expeditions, a British party led by Scott and a Norwegian one led by Roald Amundsen, were rivals for the prize. Amundsen had a flying start from his base at the Bay of Whales, while 800 kilometres (500 miles) to

Left The inside of Shackleton's hut at McMurdo Sound, as he left it after his bid to reach the South Pole in 1908.

Right Shackleton's ship *Endurance* heels over as it is literally squashed between two ice floes.

the east Scott struggled southwards from McMurdo Sound. Amundsen's team, who were experienced explorers and were not carrying heavy scientific equipment, had a relatively easy trip to the Pole. They reached it a month ahead of the British party. When Scott saw the Norwegian flag flying over the icy landscape, he was bitterly disappointed. Already greatly weakened by the outward journey, short of food and fuel, and plagued by fierce storms, the party failed to make it back to their base. Six months later their bodies were found huddled together in their last camp.

For sheer courage, one of Ernest Shackleton's expeditions was perhaps the most remarkable of all, although he never reached Antarctica. In January, 1915, his ship 'Endurance' was squashed between two huge ice floes, and the crew were forced to abandon

her. The party spent three months camped on an ice floe before they were able to make the journey by open boat to Elephant Island. At one point the floe they were on split in two, the crack passing right under one of the tents! They had no way of communicating with the outside world. Shackleton himself, with five companions, set out in an open boat to cross 1,100 kilometres (685 miles) of the stormiest seas in the world to get help. By almost a miracle they reached the island of South Georgia, and trekked across its frozen mountains to one of the whaling stations. Four relief expeditions were needed before the rest of the party were finally rescued.

Shackleton's voyage marked the end of an era in Antarctic exploration. Admiral Byrd's expedition in the 1930s made extensive use of snowmobiles and aeroplanes.

5 MODERN EXPLORATION AND RESEARCH

Today's expeditions

The chief aim of the early explorers was to make magnetic maps which show the South Magnetic Pole – that is, the place to which a compass points, not the geographical South Pole which is at 90° South. But they also made careful notes on climate, icebergs and sea ice. They began to measure the depths of various parts of the ocean and to collect and study the sea plants and animals. As soon as they reached the continent they set up observatories and also studied the rocks, ice formations, birds, penguins and seals they found around them.

Modern methods of studying the sea were introduced early this century. The German ships, *Deutschland* and *Meteor*, made maps and diagrams that tell us much of what we know about the water circulation on the Atlantic side. Another great step forward was made by the British 'Discovery Investigations' which for 20 years or more studied Antarctic whales. These expeditions also mapped the whales' food

supply, and studied water movements, plant and animal populations and the availability of nutrients in the water. (Nutrients are biochemicals produced by the decay of dead plants and animals.) They aimed at preserving the dwindling stock of Antarctic whales.

Between 1939 and 1941 the Americans showed an increased interest in Antarctic exploration. They brought in aeroplanes and tractors, and helped to outline previously unknown coastlines. After 1945, these operations were extended with the help of icebreakers. There was another leap forward in research during the International Geophysical Year (1957–8). Today, scientists and other specialists from twelve countries man 40 stations, including a large station at the Pole itself. They study the atmosphere, the Earth's magnetic field and *Aurora Australis,* the scientific term for the extraordinary 'Southern Lights'. These usually appear as streamers of many colours in the sky, especially at night, and are produced by electrical activity. The recent studies of rocks, ice, birds, plants and animals occupy hundreds of scientists.

At sea, the most remarkable advance has been in mapping the sea floor and its sediments. Deep drilling has provided new information on the formation and geological history of the ocean. Moored instruments for measuring currents and drifting floats which can be tracked by ships or satellites have added greatly to our knowledge of the water movements. New international biological studies are now being aimed at conserving krill – the small, shrimp-like animal on which whales, seals, penguins and birds feed. Krill is now threatened because it is being overfished.

Opposite Many new instruments were used during the International Geophysical Year. On the left a seismic recorder measures the thickness of the ice, while on the right an instrument is lowered to take samples from the sea floor.

Below left This instrument is measuring the strength of Antarctic tides.

Below right Biologists take marine samples.

Supplies for an expedition

Above Expedition member tucks into a king-size boiled egg. It is the egg of the wandering albatross, which takes some twenty minutes to boil and is equal in content to eight ordinary hen's eggs.

In the early days of Antarctic exploration, all the stores needed for a two to three year expedition, and all the men taking part, could be carried in one or two small ships. That is how Scott, Shackleton, Amundsen, Mawson and Byrd took their expeditions to Antarctica. But modern exploration is on a much bigger scale. Projects in Antarctica these days need big, powerful ships, aircraft, tractors, dozens of scientists, technicians and other helpers, large and well-equipped bases, and many hundreds of tonnes of stores each year. The stores include food, clothing and medical supplies for the members of the expedition, and

fuel, spare parts and replacements for the equipment. All this has to be taken down to Antarctica in good time for the start of the season's work in early spring.

Organizing supplies for a modern expedition is a big job in itself. Most expeditions have a permanent headquarters at a port in the southern hemisphere, as close as possible to Antarctica. The headquarters for the United States' expedition, 'Operation Deepfreeze', is in Christchurch, New Zealand, which has a large airport (Harewood) as well as a nearby harbour (Lyttelton). Both are important, because 'Operation Deepfreeze' uses long-distance aircraft as well as ships for supplying its Antarctic bases.

Stores for the expedition build up throughout the year in big warehouses in Christchurch. They include all kinds of supplies from light bulbs to rolling-pins, tractors to writing paper, thermometers to cans of baked beans. All these will have been ordered by the people who are already down at the bases. The items have all to be packed carefully, crated up for travel, and addressed to the right base.

In October, the first of the big, four-engined aircraft fly into Harewood from the United States, with their crews and ground staff who will keep them flying throughout the season. They load up with stores and fly down to Antarctica: a journey of 3,600 kilometres (2,250 miles) which takes seven or eight hours. The first flights always include fresh meat and vegetables, which the men at the bases have been missing all winter, and the mail-bags containing hundreds of parcels and letters that have been piling up for them in Christchurch.

Below Modern icebreaker steams through the ice pack near McMurdo Sound.

Above American naval vessels unload supplies for the men wintering in Antarctica during 'Operation Deepfreeze'.

Flights leave Christchurch almost every day in spring, taking out stores and bringing back the members of the expedition who have wintered at the bases and are due to come home. At McMurdo Sound the aircraft land on sea ice, which is three to four metres (10 to 13 ft) thick, on a specially prepared runway. From there they fly out to the smaller bases, taking stores to the permanent South Pole station 1,360 kilometres (850 miles) away, and others even farther across the Polar plateau. Landing and taking off at these high plateau stations is a tricky business, and the planes stay only long enough for the stores to be unloaded and the passengers to be dropped and picked up. They do not even shut down the engines, in case they have difficulty starting up again in the thin atmosphere and extreme cold.

In November and December the ships of 'Operation Deepfreeze' – icebreakers, tankers and cargo vessels – arrive in Lyttelton harbour. Already loaded with stores brought directly from the United States, they refuel, take on board all the extra items that are waiting at the dockside, and head south for the Antarctic. The tough, sturdy icebreakers go first; their reinforced, specially shaped bows cut a channel through the fast ice of McMurdo Sound, so that the thinner-skinned tankers and cargo vessels can follow safely through. By February, all the stores have been delivered, the ships have returned, and the aircraft are making their final flights of the year.

Below U.S. naval helicopter lands stores at an American base in Antarctica.

6 ALL ABOUT ANTARCTIC WATER

Water movements

The northern part of the Antarctic Ocean lies within the region of strong west winds (winds which blow from the west). The most ferocious storms occur between latitudes 40° and 50° South, and are known to sailors as the 'Roaring Forties'. But the wind is not always from the west; it changes direction between the north-west and the south-west. These changes of direction happen once or twice a week. Much farther south, near the continent of Antarctica, the wind blows mainly from the east, but it too changes direction between north-east and south-east.

These winds help to push along the surface water in the ocean. This means that the surface water movements are also variable, but there is an overall movement of water to the east in most of the Antarctic Ocean, and to the west farther south, close to the continent. You can see how this works on the map. Bottles with messages dropped into the ocean by sailors, and plastic drift cards put out by research ships, have travelled all round the Pole and have been picked up on beaches of

Below Research ship ploughs through heavy seas in Drake Passage – 'the windiest place on Earth'.

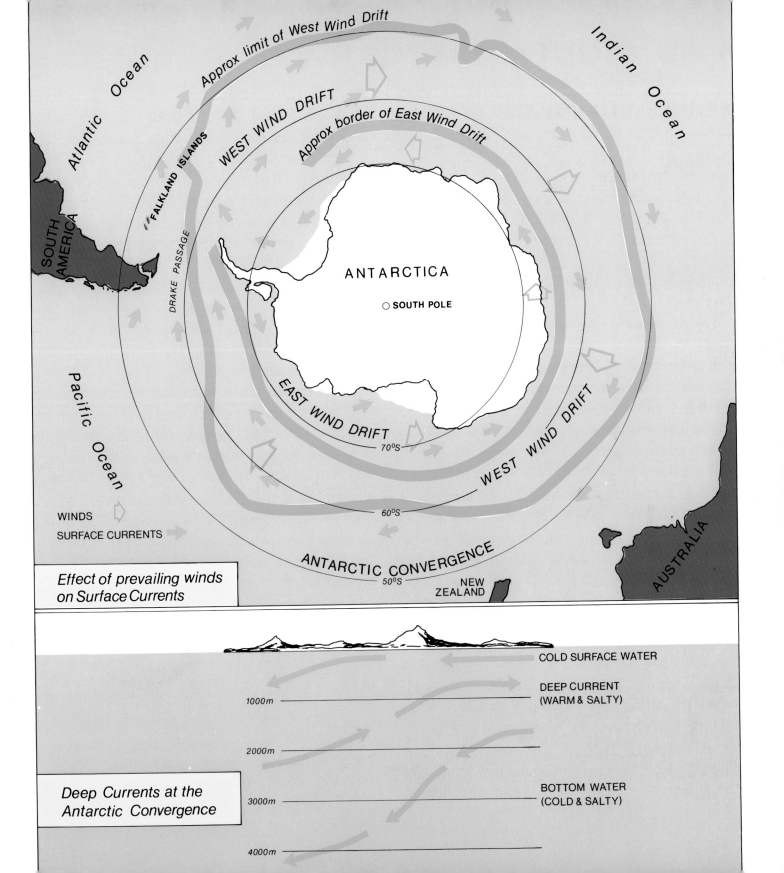

Atlantic Ocean

Indian Ocean

Approx limit of West Wind Drift

WEST WIND DRIFT

Approx border of East Wind Drift

FALKLAND ISLANDS

DRAKE PASSAGE

ANTARCTICA

○ SOUTH POLE

EAST WIND DRIFT

70°S

Pacific Ocean

WEST WIND DRIFT

60°S

WINDS

SURFACE CURRENTS

ANTARCTIC CONVERGENCE

50°S

NEW ZEALAND

AUSTRALIA

Effect of prevailing winds on Surface Currents

COLD SURFACE WATER

DEEP CURRENT (WARM & SALTY)

1000m

2000m

Deep Currents at the Antarctic Convergence

BOTTOM WATER (COLD & SALTY)

3000m

4000m

South Africa, Australia and New Zealand. They average twelve to sixteen kilometres (8 to 10 miles) a day. Near the continent, icebergs drifting in the westward current have been tracked by satellite. They average fifteen kilometres (9 miles) a day, but sometimes travel as far as 46 kilometres (29 miles) in a day. Sooner or later they drift north into the region of north-west and south-west winds where they are carried east and north until they melt.

Water movements also depend on differences in density (heaviness) of the water as well as on wind. Cold Antarctic water is heavier than the warm surface water found farther north in the Atlantic, Pacific or Indian Oceans. When it meets this warmer water it tends to sink beneath it.

We have seen that in the Antarctic Ocean there are currents at the sea surface which encircle the land. There are also currents in the water below the surface. Look at the diagram which shows a section of water from the surface to the sea floor. You will see three 'types' of water: cold Antarctic surface water, warm deep water and Antarctic bottom water. Now you can see where these different water masses go. Cold Antarctic surface water lies above warmer, deep water because the deep water is saltier and therefore heavier. This surface water has to spread east and north above the deep water which moves south to take its place. At the bottom of the ocean the Antarctic water, which is cold *and* salty, flows towards the north.

When the cold Antarctic surface water meets warmer, less dense, sub-Antarctic water, it sinks below it along what has been called the 'Antarctic Convergence'. (You can see this on the diagram.) The Antarctic Convergence is marked by a rise in temperature towards the north and a change in the types of marine plants and animals found in the water. The Antarctic Ocean is particularly rich in plant and animal life. This is because the warm deep water, which is always rich in nutrients, such as phosphate and nitrate, enriches the surface water by mixing with it.

The latest tests with special instruments and drifting floats, which measure the currents in the Antarctic, show that all the water movements are very variable. The east and west movements are complicated by large eddies (which are slow, circular water movements) sometimes 100 kilometres (60 miles) across. The exact position of the Antarctic Convergence may therefore vary at different times by this amount.

Right The plentiful marine life found in the Antarctic Ocean makes it a rich hunting ground for fishing vessels.

Waves and tides

The albatross and the round-the-world yachtsman prefer to travel from west to east because they know the wind in most of the Antarctic Ocean blows that way too. Between latitudes 40° South and 60° South lie the windiest places on Earth. There is no land to stop them, and so the winds blow throughout the year, varying their direction a little at times, and sometimes reaching speeds of 200 kilometres per hour (125 m.p.h.).

Sailors also know of the dangerously high waves which these winds create and drive. These waves are at their most ferocious as they funnel through the Drake Passage around Cape Horn. Swell (long, rolling waves which do not break) from these storms spreads north into other oceans. This swell has been traced as far as Alaska. It also spreads south through the ice, where it can be seen on otherwise glassy seas.

Icebergs are affected by sea movements. As they break up on their way northwards through the stormy seas, they may be carved into fantastic shapes by the waves, and they also move slowly up and down with the tides. Although these movements are hard to see, they can be measured with special equipment. You can read more about icebergs on p. 20.

Many expeditions have measured the tides at their bases on the Antarctic continent. Modern instruments which can sit on the sea-bed for many weeks at a time can also be used. These show that sometimes there is only one tide a day, while at other times there are two tides. Tides are produced by the gravitational forces of the Moon and the Sun together with the spinning of the Earth. It was once thought that all tides were generated in the Antarctic Ocean, from where they spread like the swell. Although it now seems that tides are created in all oceans, the way in which they connect through the Antarctic Ocean is important to people who study tidal behaviour.

Right Early sailing vessel runs through a narrow passage in the pack-ice during a snow storm. Frequent storms and icebergs make the Antarctic Seas some of the most dangerous in the world.

Below Huge sculptured iceberg drifts around Antarctica. They are often carved into fantastic shapes by the waves.

7 LIFE IN THE OCEAN

Plankton and Antarctic krill

We have already seen how the water circulates in the Antarctic Ocean. As it moves it carries many of the things that are essential to marine life. Let's just consider what these are.

All plants, whether on land or in the sea, require carbon dioxide and water. In the presence of chlorophyll (the green pigment in plants) and sunlight, these react together to form carbohydrates and oxygen. This process is called photosynthesis. Carbon dioxide is a gas which dissolves readily in water, and so there is very rarely any shortage of it. But what about sunlight? We have seen that near the Poles in the summer there are 24 hours of daylight and that during the winter there are 24 hours of darkness. Photosynthesis can therefore only occur during the summer.

Sea ice in the Antarctic Ocean acts like an enormous curtain stopping light entering the water. This also restricts photosynthesis. Even where there is no ice, sunlight does not penetrate very far down into the water and

Below Some of the extraordinary shapes of phytoplankton when seen under a microscope. These tiny plants are a very important food source for other marine creatures.

Above Krill swarm in the Antarctic. These small shrimp-like crustaceans often mass in huge numbers. They feed on the phytoplankton near the surface of the sea and are in turn eaten by whales and other marine life.

photosynthesis only takes place in the top 10 to 50 metres (30 to 165 ft) of the Ocean.

Plants also require nutrients. These nutrients are dissolved in the water and are brought to the surface by the movement of the water. Phytoplankton are microscopic plants found in the sea. In the Antarctic, these plants are produced in enormous numbers in surface water during the summer months. Few are more than one millimetre across and many have spiky or feathery projections which slow down the rate at which they sink through the water. One common group of phytoplankton is the diatoms, but there are other groups. All are different shapes and sizes.

There are probably well over 1,000 million tonnes of phytoplankton produced every year over the whole 36 million square kilometres (14 million sq. miles) of the Antarctic Ocean. Where the currents bring nutrients to the surface, and there is plenty of sunlight, the phytoplankton multiply very rapidly and form the food of zooplankton, which are tiny drifting animals.

There are all sorts of different types of small animals that are collectively called zooplankton. These include some types of jellyfish, worms, sea squirts and larval fish. The largest group is the crustaceans – animals with strange names such as copepods or amphipods (which are related to the sandhoppers found on the beach) and also Antarctic krill.

The Antarctic krill, or to give it its scientific name *Euphausia superba* (so as not to confuse it with krill from other oceans) is found all over the Antarctic Ocean south of the Antarctic Convergence. They are small, shrimp-like animals which grow to a maximum size of about six centimetres (3 in.). They feed on the phytoplankton which they filter out of the water with their feathery forelimbs. It is not only the zooplankton that filter their food from the water, but also larger marine animals such as some whales, seals and birds.

The krill have a habit of swimming together in large shoals or swarms. These swarms have over 30,000 krill in each cubic metre of water and the swarms themselves may extend for tens or even thousands of metres. Many larger animals – whales, seals, birds, squid and fish – feed on krill and other forms of marine life. A common group of fish is the ice fish. Ice fish are the only vertebrates that do not have a red blood pigment *(haemoglobin)* to carry oxygen around their bodies. You would recognize an ice fish because its gills are white and not red.

Below Young southern right whale. These whales swim south to the Antarctic in the spring to feed on the huge swarms of krill.

Above Ice fish can survive in near freezing water.

Life near the sea floor

For most of the year the water temperature of the Antarctic Ocean hovers around zero. You might expect that very few animals would be happy to live under these harsh conditions, and although there are many birds and seals, the Antarctic sea shores are certainly rather bare compared with those in the warmer regions of the world. But the reason is not so much the low temperatures, but rather the crushing and grinding effect of ice and icebergs as they pound and scrape the shore and the sea-bed immediately below it.

A few metres beneath the surface, however, beyond the reach of the ice, life on the Antarctic sea-bed is as rich, or even richer, than in other oceans of the world. For the large amount of plant plankton living in the surface waters is a food source for the enormous swarms of krill on which the great whales feed. Indirectly, the plankton also provides plenty of food for the bottom-living animals, because of what is known as the 'food chain'. This means

Below These strange bottom-living creatures are called nemertine worms. Some species have a long trunk which is used to catch other small animals for food.

Above This sea spider has very long legs and a tiny body, and crawls about on the sea floor in search of its prey.

that some creatures are eaten by others which in turn are the food of other animals.

Much of the Antarctic sea-bed is carpeted with thick mud made up of the glass-like skeletons of millions of tiny plants and animals which have fallen to the bottom after they have died. In and on this mud live large populations of animals including sponges, sea anemones, molluscs, crabs, worms and starfishes. All of these animals have to be able to withstand the very low temperatures, of course, and they are not the same types which are found in the much warmer, shallow waters in the tropics. Some Antarctic animals are found only in this region, although many of them may be found *deeper down* in the temperate and tropical seas where the water is just as cold as it is in the Antarctic. Both Antarctic and Arctic animals spread to the deeper waters of the tropics, so that in some cases the same, or very similar, shallow-living animals are found near both Poles, but not in the warmer surface waters between.

45

8 WHALES, SEALS AND BIRDS

Whales

In the spring and summer, the Antarctic Ocean is the feeding ground of the great baleen (whalebone) whales. These whales live during the rest of the year in warmer waters where they mate and, about a year later, give birth to their calves. They swim southwards each spring to feed on the swarms of krill which live in the surface waters of Antarctic seas.

Baleen whales have no teeth. Instead they use the several hundred horny plates hanging down from the sides of the roofs of their mouths as a filter. These baleen plates have dense, inner fringes of hairy bristles which sieve the krill from the sea as the whale fills its mouth. The whales spend the summer feeding and building up a thick layer of fat (blubber) under their skin, before swimming northwards again in the autumn. The blubber provides energy for their winter stay in warmer waters where most whales feed very little.

There are several different kinds of baleen whales. The blue whale is the world's largest animal. It can grow to a length of nearly 30 metres (100 ft) and weigh about 130 tonnes. Other kinds are the fin, humpback and minke whales.

The blubber of baleen whales provides whalers with oil from which margarine and soap can be made. Whalemeat provides human and animal food, and their bones yield meal for animal food and fertilizers. The numbers of some kinds of whales, including blue and humpback whales, have been very much reduced because too many were caught by whalers before the catches were properly controlled. These whales are now protected and it is hoped that their numbers will increase again. Catches of other Antarctic whales are also controlled to prevent too many being killed.

Above Minke whale diving. All whales breathe in air at the surface and can sometimes remain underwater for as long as an hour.

Left Early whaling ship at anchor in Antarctic waters.

Below Blue whale's carcass being cut up on South Georgia. Today the blue whale is in danger of extinction.

Seals

Seals are characteristic animals of polar seas and more than half of all the seals in the world live in the Antarctic. They are mammals that are adapted to life in the sea but must still return to the shore, or to floating ice, to give birth. You are most likely to see seals when they are out of the water, but it is in the water that they catch their food, and they can swim with wonderful grace.

There are six sorts of seal in the Antarctic.

By far the most common is the crab-eater seal. Despite its name, this seal does not feed on crabs but on krill – the food of whales and many sea birds. Crab-eaters are found singly or in small groups in areas of loose pack-ice. Many of them bear scars, which are the result of encounters with leopard seals.

Weddell seals are most common near the shore or in regions of fast ice. They are often found in quite large groups, but do not lie close

Below A scientist warily greets an angry bull elephant seal. These huge seals average two or three tonnes in weight and, although very agile in the water, are very slow-moving on land.

Above The leopard seal is a solitary animal, often found on ice floes in the outer regions of the ice pack.

to each other. Weddell seals feed on fish and squid, which they can catch at great depths. In winter they keep breathing holes open in the ice by gnawing at it with their teeth.

Leopard seals are widely distributed in the Antarctic and are occasionally seen in the Falkland Islands. They are large solitary seals that have earned a bad reputation because they are often seen preying on penguins near their rookeries. In fact they feed mainly on krill and at times on young crab-eater seals.

Ross seals are the rarest of the Antarctic seals. They live in areas of dense pack-ice, and so are hardly ever seen. They feed on squid and fish.

Elephant seals are the largest of all seals: a big male can weigh up to four tonnes. They are found on the sub-Antarctic islands in immense herds in the spring. It is then that each bull (male) assembles a large harem of cows (females) which it will defend from its aggressive male neighbours.

Fur seals were nearly exterminated in the last century, but they are now protected animals and are recovering fast. A flourishing colony exists at South Georgia. They are eared seals, like the familiar sea lion. Like elephant seals, the fur seal bulls are much bigger than the cows and keep harems in the breeding season. Fur seals feed on krill.

Antarctic birds

Of all the Antarctic birds, penguins and albatrosses are the best known.

Penguins cannot fly. On land they are clumsy and stand upright, but in the water they swim very well using their paddle-like wings.

Several sorts of penguin live in the Antarctic Ocean. Macaroni penguins have golden crests on their heads. Chinstrap penguins have a black band across their white chin which looks like the strap of a helmet. Adélie penguins have black heads and white rings around their eyes so they always look surprised. King penguins, which you can see in zoos, are related to emperor penguins. Most of these penguins nest in rookeries on islands in the Antarctic Ocean or on the shores of Antarctica. Emperor penguins breed on the fast ice around the continent.

Emperors are the biggest penguins. They never stray far from the Antarctic continent. In the early winter, each female lays a single, large egg. She gives it to the male then goes away to sea to feed. As there is no nest, he carries the egg balanced on his feet. He covers the egg with folds of loose skin to keep it warm. During the winter it is very cold, so all the males huddle together to avoid freezing to death. After two months the female returns and the egg hatches. The male is now free to find his first meal for months. The parents continue to carry the chick until it gets too big. At five months old, the chick goes off to sea.

Albatrosses are huge birds with long, narrow wings. They are marvellous fliers and

gliders. The wandering albatross is the biggest albatross, and has a wingspan of 3.5 metres (11.5 ft). Wandering albatrosses produce one egg every other year, and may live for forty years.

Other birds living in the Antarctic Ocean include petrels and skuas. Petrels are like albatrosses but are mostly much smaller. There are many different sorts of petrels. Skuas look like brown seagulls. They steal the eggs and chicks of other birds.

Left Adelie penguins line up for a plunge in the sea.

Below right Black-brow albatross on nest with chick. The small dark streaks around its eyes give it a characteristic frowning appearance.

Below left In the spring, the beaches of many sub-Antarctic islands are invaded by a jostling crowd of nesting penguins.

Above An expedition member drags a sledge over a crevasse during a British survey of the coasts of South Georgia in 1952.

Cold, windswept islands

Halfway to Antarctica, widely scattered across the stormy ocean, lie the sub-Antarctic islands. A long way from each other and from the rest of the world, the dozen or so groups of sub-Antarctic islands are for most people little more than names on the map. Some, like Tristan da Cunha and the Falkland Islands, have populations which live there all the time. Others such as the Marion Islands, the Crozets and Kerguelen, St Paul, Amsterdam, Macquarie and Campbell Island, have small scientific bases, and others again are completely deserted except for the seals and sea birds. From the sea in summer these islands look green and inviting, but sailors and scientists who know the sub-Antarctic islands know that the winters are cold and dreary. Among sailors they have a fearsome reputation, for the seas around them are the stormiest in the world, and dozens of ships have been wrecked on their uncharted rocks and reefs.

The warmer sub-Antarctic islands lie in the westerlies – strong winds that blow constantly all the year round, raising mighty seas that beat against their western shores. Buffeting gales, low, scurrying clouds, lashing rain and snow make up their climate. Always wet in summer, they are usually snow-blanketed in winter, and the larger islands have permanent snow and ice on their mountain tops, with glaciers sweeping down to sea level. These islands are covered with grass, including

Above Nesting gentoo penguins amongst ice floes.

tussock-grasses that may grow taller than a man. Further south lie the colder sub-Antarctic islands, covered with snow for much of the year and supporting only patches of mosses, lichens and grasses.

In summer the beaches of these islands are thronged with seals, and their cliffs and uplands support enormous populations of sea birds, including penguins and petrels. The seals and birds feed at sea, but come ashore to breed in their thousands.

The Falkland Islands

The Falkland Islands are the biggest group of sub-Antarctic Islands. They lie 480 kilometres (300 miles) east of South America. There are two main islands – East and West Falkland – with about 400 smaller islets surrounding them. Just over 1,900 people live on the Falklands, most of them on the two main islands. About half of the population live in the one town – Stanley, the capital.

The Falklands are a low-lying group of islands, with a total area of about 16,000 square kilometres (6200 sq. miles). The highest hills rise just above 700 metres (2,310 ft). Much of the ground is covered with wet, springy turf, overlying thick beds of peat. When first discovered in the late seventeenth century, the Falklands were uninhabited. French, Spanish and British settlers arrived at various times, but only the British settlements survived. The populations of these islands

Below Sea-plane lands with supplies at one of the outlying islands in the Falklands.

Above Bleak, windswept moors on the Falkland Islands.

increased from the mid-nineteenth century onwards as more and more of the land was put to grazing. Now the Falkland Islands are divided into farms and ranches for cattle and sheep. About half the population tends the livestock, and farm products – especially sheep's wool – bring their prosperity.

As they are separated by many waterways and sea channels, and because they have very few roads, it is difficult to travel around and between the Falkland Islands. Sheep and cattle are carried to the outlying islands by boat for summer grazing, and small sea-planes carry the islanders from their farms to the capital. Most of the outlying settlements are linked by telephone and radio, and the planes can be turned into ambulances to bring sick and injured people into the Stanley Hospital. Travelling teachers visit schoolchildren in the outlying settlements, and there are also boarding schools for the older children. Though isolated and remote from the rest of the world, the Falkland Islanders have made a good life for themselves.

10 RESOURCES OF THE ANTARCTIC OCEAN

Above Fur seals almost became extinct in the nineteenth century due to over-hunting. They are now protected animals and their numbers are recovering fast.

Fur seals were the first Antarctic resource to be exploited. Several million were killed just for their skins – in fact so many were killed that by 1820 they were almost extinct. Even in 1930 only about 30 fur seals were seen on South Georgia. But now there are very many more in that area – possibly half a million.

Next, the whales were harvested. The harpoon gun and then the floating factory-ships made it possible to hunt the great whales over much of the Antarctic Ocean. Controls have now been applied which restrict fishing for some species and forbid it completely for others. If all countries keep to these regulations the numbers of whales should now increase.

Nowadays, fishermen go to the Antarctic to catch krill and fish. Large factory trawlers are equipped with echo sounders that detect krill swarms. They also have special trawl nets to catch them and so can land hundreds of tonnes in a season. Several food products are made from krill: krill meal (to feed pigs), krill paste, krill cheese and whole peeled krill. At the moment, the total world catch of krill of a hundred thousand tonnes is not large when compared to the amount known to be present in the Antarctic Ocean. It is not just human beings, however, who are interested in eating krill. Whales, seals, birds, squid and fish all feed on it to some extent, and so if we take too much, we will deprive these other krill-eaters of food. Let us hope that the fishing industry has learned from its mistakes with the whales

Above Whaler with its catch. A total ban on whaling is now needed if some of the species of great whale are to survive.

Right Trawling for krill in the Antarctic. Krill must not be over-fished, or marine life which depends on krill for food will suffer.

and seals, and that it will now manage krill-fishing sensibly and so maintain the krill and all the creatures dependent on it indefinitely.

During this century there has been a rapid increase in the amount of fuel used throughout the world. Coal, oil and natural gas are being extracted from the earth in increasingly greater quantities. A few years ago, the bulk of the world's oil came from wells drilled on land – the technology was too basic and the cost too high

Above Oceanographic sampling bottle. Scientists use this instrument to test the saltiness, oxygen content and temperature of sea-water at various depths in the ocean.

to drill out at sea. But today, off-shore oil and gas drilling is commonplace in many parts of the world.

We know that oil, natural gas and coal are all present in the Antarctic. At this stage we do not know the extent of these resources. The continental shelf in the Antarctic is deeper than those in other parts of the world. The weather can be very bad for long periods and icebergs could easily damage drilling platforms. All these factors would contribute to making the cost of recovering oil and gas from the Antarctic very expensive. But the price of these resources all over the world is continually rising, and it may soon become economical to extract them from the Antarctic.

Water is another important resource in the Antarctic. As we have seen, Antarctic ice moves in the form of glaciers, and ice shelves are formed. Where these meet the sea, large chunks (icebergs) break off and drift northwards. Some large companies are proposing to tow icebergs from the Antarctic Ocean to the coasts of dry, barren areas of the world so that the fresh water can be used to irrigate the land and allow farmers to grow crops. The presence of the icebergs close to these dry regions might also change the climate locally and keep the land of the area fertile.

We must also remember that the Antarctic, its land, ice, plants and animals, is of interest to tourists as well as to industrialists and scientists. Touring the Antarctic in ships, and more recently in aeroplanes, is now quite common.

Above Large freshwater iceberg. Scientists have suggested that icebergs could be towed to dry areas of the world and used for irrigation.

The vast landmass of Antarctica does not belong to any country. Nor do the seas around it. Seven nations have long-standing claims to parts of it, but these claims are not recognized by other nations active in the area. There is a large area not claimed at all. Antarctica has long been of interest to scientists and explorers from a fairly small number of countries.

The beginning of large-scale co-operation between scientists from many countries was during the International Geophysical Year (1957–8). Scientists from twelve nations including Britain, America and Russia, worked together on the Antarctic programmes for this large, concentrated international study of the globe. This led them to form an international 'Scientific Committee on Antarctic Research' of the International Council of Scientific Unions. Its aims were to continue to promote international collaboration in the planning of future research.

In 1959, the twelve governments whose scientists had worked together signed a special Antarctic Treaty. This stated that they would continue to co-operate in supporting research and to preserve Antarctica and the seas around it for peaceful purposes. While the Treaty is in force all national territorial claims are frozen, and scientists from Treaty nations can work anywhere in the area.

During the 1960s, research continued to progress well and governments agreed on measures to conserve plants and animals. This included setting aside a number of 'Specially Protected Areas'.

The nations which agreed on the Antarctic Treaty still want as much as ever to protect this unique region and to encourage research there. Recently, however, they have had to think carefully about living resources, such as fish and krill. What happens if we take too much fish from the Antarctic? Already fishing trawlers from many countries come to this area. And they also have to think about other resources which may be found there in the future – oil for example (see p. 57). If oil is found beneath the land or the sea, what effect will its exploitation have on Antarctica which has so far remained unspoiled?

In the future, governments of various nations must try to find ways in which any resources from the Antarctic can be used to help mankind. At the same time they must ensure that we do not spoil the area by taking too much of a particular resource or by polluting the land or sea. At present the Antarctic Ocean is very clean.

The past co-operation of many countries working together for these purposes despite their different views on many other issues, has been a fine example to the world. There is a

Left The flags of many nations show where national expeditions have sought to discover the secrets of Antarctica.

Above A penguin called 'Flipper' became the mascot of a United States expedition to Antarctica in 1958. He was even given his own naval uniform.

Right Divers work from small boats to obtain marine samples from the sea-bed.

Above A United States Aircraft, equipped with skis, takes off from the South Pole. Ice crystals and the jet-assisted take-off apparatus form a trailing cloud of smoke and ice fog.

great need for scientists to continue to co-operate during the coming years in the study of the Antarctic. In this way we can improve our knowledge of this huge area and try to provide answers to important questions which might affect our future.

It is not yet possible to judge how much fish or krill can be taken from the sea without disturbing the balance of nature. It is not known for certain if there is oil under the sea floor near the coast, nor, if there is, what would be the consequences of extracting it. There is still much to learn about the effect of the huge amounts of ice present in the Antarctic, on weather in other parts of the world. But it is not only these issues which are important to scientists. Much research is still needed into all the basic natural sciences of glaciology (the study of ice), geology, biology and physics if we want to improve our understanding of this vast and little-known region, and so of the planet on which we live.

Above Measuring Antarctic cod aboard a marine research vessel.

Glossary

Antarctic Circle   Line of latitude at 66° 32′ South. Along this line there are 24 hours of daylight on Midsummer Day and 24 hours of darkness on Midwinter Day.

Antarctic Convergence   The region where cold Antarctic surface water meets warmer, sub-Antarctic water and sinks below it.

Antarctic Ocean   General term given to the seas surrounding the continent of Antarctica.

Aurora Australis   The 'Southern Lights'. Seen as streamers of different colours in the sky, especially at night. They are similar to *Aurora Borealis* which occurs at the North Pole.

Blizzard   Blinding snow storm, especially one where powdery snow is swept up from the ground by a high wind.

Blubber   Layer of fat beneath the skin of whales.

Continental drift   The movement of landmasses of the world towards or away from each other.

Continental shelf   That part of a continent which lies off-shore and is covered by a shallow layer of water or, in the case of the Antarctic, ice.

Continental slope   The slope which joins the end of the continental shelf with the deeper part of the ocean.

Crustacean   Animal (usually living in the sea) with hard shell and many legs. Prawns, crabs and lobsters are all crustaceans.

Current   The flow of water in any given direction.

Fast ice   Frozen sea-water found in sheltered, coastal waters.

Fossil   The remains, impression or trace of a plant or animal found preserved in rock.

Glacier   A huge mass of ice that moves extremely slowly down a mountainside.

Glaciology   The scientific study of ice.

Iceberg   Large mass of ice which has broken off an ice shelf. It is made up of fresh water and can be found drifting among pack-ice.

Icebreaker   Ship which has been reinforced to allow it to force a passage through pack-ice and fast ice.

Ice floe   Chunk of pack-ice broken off by the action of waves.

Ice shelf   Vast floating sheet of ice on some parts of the coast, fed by glaciers descending from the mountains.

Krill   Small, shrimp-like animals which form the main food of many whales, seals, penguins and other birds. Antarctic krill is a special species known as *Euphausia superba*.

Latitude   Lines of latitude are imaginary circles around the Earth. They are measured in degrees north and south of the Equator.

Lava   Molten rock which flows down the sides of a volcano, then cools and solidifies.

Mollusc   A soft animal without a backbone, such as an octopus or a squid. Some molluscs (mussels, snails, whelks) have a protective shell.

Nutrients   Biochemicals (e.g. nitrate, phosphate) present in sea-water and produced by the decay of dead plants and animals.

Pack-ice   Frozen sea-water which drifts with the winds and tides.

Plankton   Tiny animals (zooplankton) and plants (phytoplankton) which drift in millions through the seas.

Polar plateau   3,000-metre high plateau leading to the South Pole.

Pollution   Contamination of sea-water by dangerous chemicals from industry, oil spillage and sewage or other rubbish.

'Roaring Forties'   Fierce westerly gales which occur between latitudes 40° and 50° South.

Sediments   Clay, sand and silt which collect on the sea

Left Scott's ship H.M.S. *Discovery*.

floor and may become hard rocks. Remains of dead animals are also incorporated into the sediments.

Silt Fine sand and fertile soil washed down to the sea by rivers.

South Magnetic Pole The point to which a compass is attracted and which is some distance from the geographical South Pole. It varies from year to year as the Earth's magnetic field changes.

South Pole The permanently fixed geographical point (90° South) around which the Earth rotates.

Sub-Antarctic Describing the seas and islands outside the Antarctic Circle but south of Australia, Africa and South America. Sub-Antarctic water meets Antarctic water along the Antarctic Convergence.

Swell Heaving of the sea, with long, rolling waves which do not break. Swell is common after a storm.

Tides The rise and fall of the surface of the sea which depends on the attraction of the Sun and the Moon. In the Antarctic there may be one or two tides in a day.

Tussock-grass Tall-growing, stout grass common in the Falkland Islands and other sub-Antarctic regions.

Books to read

Angel, M. and H., *Ocean Life* (Octopus Books)

Cochrane, J., *The Amazing World of the Sea* (Angus & Robertson)

Keeling, C. H., *Under the Sea* (F. Watts)

Lambert, D., *The Oceans* (Ward Lock)

Merret, N., *The How and Why Wonder Book of the Deep Sea* (Transworld)

Parsons, J., *Oceans* (Macdonald Educational)

Saunders, G. D., *Spotters' Guide to Seashells* (Usborne)

Stonehouse, B., *The Living World of the Sea* (Hamlyn)

The people who wrote this book

Pat Hargreaves   Marine biologist, Institute of Oceanographic Sciences, Surrey (General Editor).

Sir George Deacon   Former Director of the Institute of Oceanographic Sciences, Surrey.

Dr Roger Searle   Marine geophysicist, Institute of Oceanographic Sciences, Surrey.

Dr Gordon Robin   Geophysicist. Director, Scott Polar Research Institute, University of Cambridge.

Margaret B. Deacon   Historian and writer. Visiting Fellow, Institute for Advanced Studies in the Humanities, University of Edinburgh.

Dr Bernard Stonehouse   Biologist and specialist in marine birds and animals. Senior Lecturer, University of Bradford.

Dr David Pugh   Principal Scientific Officer, Institute of Oceanographic Sciences, Merseyside.

Dr Inigo Everson   Marine biologist, British Antarctic Survey, Cambridge.

Dr Tony Rice   Marine biologist, Institute of Oceanographic Sciences, Surrey.

Dr Sidney G. Brown   Zoologist. Principal Scientific Officer, Sea Mammal Research Unit, British Antarctic Survey, Cambridge.

W. Nigel Bonner   Biologist. Head, Life Sciences Division, British Antarctic Survey, Cambridge.

Michael H. Thurston   Zoologist. Principal Scientific Officer, Institute of Oceanographic Sciences, Surrey.

G. E. Hemmen   Executive Secretary, Scientific Committee on Antarctic Research, Cambridge.

Picture acknowledgements

British Antarctic Survey 9, 14, 16, 17, 26, 29 (both), 31, 41, 43, 45, 47 (below), 49, 51, 53, 55, 56, 57 (above), 58, 59; Bruce Coleman, by the following photographers: Jen & Des Bartlett *front cover*, 23, 34, 42, 53, 54; Francesco Erize 6, 20–21, 38–39; Inigo Everson 57, 63, 65; M. P. Harris 50–51 (above); Gordon Williamson 47; Geoslides 19 (below); Tim Gill 10–11; Eric and David Hosking/D. P. Wilson 40; Anna Jupp 13; Keystone 19 (above); John Mitchell 15, 35; Seaphot 44; Bernard Stonehouse 7, 33; John Topham 8 (bottom), 12, 21, 24, 25 (both), 28, 30, 32, 37, 46, 48, 50–51 (below), 52, 60, 62, 64; Wayland Picture Library 8 (above), 22, 27, 39 (above), 66; Zefa *title page*.

Index